W9-CZL-224

MAKING THEMES WORK

Distributed by
Vernon Teach and Learn
Tel. (604) 545-3611

Vernon T+L   Dec 93   15.00

MAKING THEMES WORK

ANNE DAVIES

•

CAREN CAMERON

•

COLLEEN POLITANO

PEGUIS PUBLISHERS
WINNIPEG • CANADA

Printed and bound in Canada by Hignell Printing Limited

97 96 95 94 93 5 4 3 2 1

Canadian Cataloguing in Publication Data
Davies, Anne, 1955–

  Making themes work

  (Building connections)
  Includes bibliographical references.
  ISBN 1-895411-60-2

1. Curriculum planning.   I. Cameron, Caren, 1949–
II. Politano, Colleen, 1946–   III. Title.
IV. Series.

LB2806.15.D39 1993   375'.001   C93-098063-8

Book and Cover Design: Laura Ayers

Peguis Publishers Ltd.
520 Hargrave Street
Winnipeg, MB
Canada R3A 0X8

This book is dedicated to the teachers and children
with whom we have worked. We have been consistently delighted,
amazed, and inspired as they have made the connections necessary
for their own teaching and learning.

CONTENTS

ACKNOWLEDGMENTS

Although this book bears the name of three authors, no book is ever written by the authors alone. We'd like to acknowledge those who have supported us in our efforts and influenced our thinking.

We have enjoyed having conversations with and know our thinking has been enriched by Brian Cambourne, Yetta Goodman, Ken Goodman, Jerome Harste, Terry Johnson, Daphne Louis, Norma Mickelson, Judith Newman, Alison Preece, and Frank Smith.

We recognize and appreciate the willingness of Colleen's teaching partners to create classroom environments, which produced many of the samples and photographs. Our thanks to Jennifer Davidson, Karen Leeson, and Linda Silverthorne. We are appreciative of Edna Knight's agreement to let us share part of her overview—see pages 23 and 24.

Finally, we would like to recognize our families and friends who encouraged and supported us and put up with the inconvenience of long writing weekends. In particular our thanks to Sheena, Mackenzie, and Stewart Duncan; Wayne King; and Leon Politano.

INTRODUCTION

WHO IS THIS BOOK FOR?

Making Themes Work is intended for busy teachers who are trying
to make sense of the many changes taking place in education today.
Centering learning around themes can be an excellent way to
enhance learning in the classroom. This book can serve as a starting
point for those teachers who are using themes for the first time. And
for those who have been using themes for many years, it can help to
expand their repertoire of strategies for developing and working
with themes, as well as to confirm their successes.

This book includes

- ☛ innovative starting points for developing themes
- ☛ effective ways for children to show what they know
- ☛ powerful evaluation strategies for children and teachers
- ☛ specific suggestions for communicating effectively with
  colleagues, parents, and administrators
- ☛ practical suggestions for managing and organizing themes

Although there are other books about themes, this may be the last
one you need to buy on this topic. Once you construct your own
knowledge around using themes and how themes can best work for
you and for your children, you won't need to look to outside experts
to give you the answers. This book is an invitation to recognize the
expert within each of us.

WHAT IS A THEME?

That depends on who is talking about it. When we asked colleagues
the question, "What is a theme?" we got answers that ranged from
"a one-week study on bears" to "a critical issue affecting the lives
of everyone on the planet." Some teachers talked about a theme as
being "a thread that ties together all aspects of the curriculum."
Others said, "a theme frees children to work independently." All
agreed that a theme can serve as a vehicle that allows children to
develop a sense of shared understanding.

When we looked up the word *theme* in a few dictionaries, the definitions that appeared most frequently were *a recurring, unifying idea;
topic under discussion; stem; common element; question; problem; concept;
main idea; matter at hand;* and *gist.*

When we tried to define *theme*—as we use the term for educational purposes—we thought that all of the definitions given had merit. We realized that if we had been asked the question, "What is a theme?" five years ago, our response would have been very different from what it is today. Our understanding of what a theme is or what a theme can be has evolved as we have grown and learned. (This may have happened for you too.) We also know that once an ever-so-definitive definition is provided, it tends to close down our learning. In this book, we describe themes rather than define them. We believe that only you, within your context, can develop a useful definition of what a theme is.

It has been our experience that the use of a theme in a classroom begins when we—teachers, children, or both—agree on the choice of a subject, an idea, or a concept around which to organize learning experiences. We know that there are themes that never get off the ground, themes that fly, and themes that sputter and die. Some themes continue for a month or more while others are over in two days. Themes can be about something as specific as "penguins" or as broad as "change." The value of using a theme is not measured by the time involved, the number of subject areas that are integrated, or the relative merit of the topic; the value is in the learning that takes place. When a particular focus becomes an integrated, relevant, and connected learning experience for you and your children, you have created a theme.

ARTICULATING OUR BELIEFS— USING THEMES MAKES SENSE

WHAT DO WE KNOW ABOUT LEARNERS?

With all the changes happening in education today, teachers have all sorts of "pieces" from which to choose—cooperative learning, hands-on science, whole language, math manipulatives, critical thinking, writing process, and many more. We are often not sure how they fit together—it sometimes seems as though educators are going off in a million different directions. It's important to ask ourselves, "What do all of these pieces have in common?"

When teachers describe their successes in their classrooms, the same words and phrases come up again and again. When classroom experiences are successful, they say, their children are

- ☛ starting by building on what they already know
- ☛ feeling good about themselves and their work
- ☛ able to make some choices
- ☛ showing what they know in different ways
- ☛ feeling a sense of accomplishment
- ☛ working together and by themselves
- ☛ knowing that what they say is valued by their teachers and their classmates
- ☛ finding out that they can learn from others and that others can learn from them
- ☛ finding out that they have something to offer others
- ☛ seeing teachers as learners
- ☛ having fun learning
- ☛ excited about sharing with others what they are doing
- ☛ talking about what they are doing and how they are doing it

Current research confirms that how children learn parallels teachers' descriptions of successful learning experiences. Combining what the researchers are reporting about their findings with what teachers are saying about their successes, the evidence is clear. Learning is not dependent upon age or what is being learned. We know that effective learning takes place when students

- ☛ want to learn and need to learn
- ☛ realize what they have learned
- ☛ enjoy what they are doing
- ☛ can relate what they are doing to their total experience

- are allowed to take risks
- feel a sense of support
- talk about their new knowledge with others
- feel good about themselves
- have opportunities to work with others
- get to make some decisions
- have a chance to touch, smell, see, hear, feel, think

What do you believe about learners?

These same characteristics apply whether we are talking about children learning to read or write, learning math, learning science, or learning about their world.

All teachers have beliefs about learners. When teachers can articulate their beliefs clearly, they are able to screen every element of their practice by asking whether or not their practices are in alignment with their beliefs.

HOW DO THEMES FACILITATE LEARNING?

The primary purpose of using themes is to promote learning. When we asked ourselves which themes had worked for us, we realized that successful themes share many qualities: they are relevant, connected, fun, purposeful, provide for choice, and integrate different subjects. Themes work best when we consider the total needs of our children and use the themes to invite new learning.

Relevance is important because all people learn when something has meaning for them.

Themes are relevant when they give teachers ways to organize learning experiences based on their children's interests, needs, and abilities. Themes increase in relevance when children are given the opportunity to represent their knowledge in a variety of ways.

Connections are important because learning is more lasting and significant when we can integrate what we are learning with what we already know.

Themes give teachers ways to identify and invite connections between kids and topics, kids and kids, classes and classes, school and the community, old knowledge and new knowledge, and process and content. The shared experience of constructing knowledge through a theme gives learners opportunities to connect with one another.

Fun is essential. When learning is joyful, people think of it with pleasure and want to learn more and more.

Feeling a sense of accomplishment, realizing that you discovered something you didn't know before, having a shared purpose, and finding out that you can learn from others and that others can learn from you—that is fun.

We learn when we know there is a real purpose to what we are doing.

The interest stimulated by a theme and our commitment either to others or to ourselves provide real purposes for doing and for learning. When students are writing letters, preparing interviews, practicing skills, and constructing knowledge for an audience other than the teachers, the real purpose for learning is enhanced.

Choice, in project topic, selection of working partners, or ways of representing what has been learned, allows for ownership because it respects the uniqueness of each individual.

Having a choice is a powerful motivator for learners. Themes provide a way to have a common focus while allowing students to build upon their own strengths, interests, and experiences.

Integration of subjects is natural. Themes offer us a way to erase the lines that schools have created within and among subjects.

Learning is easier when we see patterns and relationships between what we know and what we seek to understand. People learn by making connections, and our ability to connect is enhanced when we see the larger context for what is being learned. A pattern illustrated by numbers in mathematics may be easier to understand and to appreciate when seen in nature as, for example, a honeycomb, a snowflake, or a rock crystal.

Why do you want to use themes?

DECIDING ON A THEME—
LOOKING AHEAD

When we decide to use a theme to structure the learning in our classrooms, we ask ourselves a number of questions that help us determine the value of a particular theme for our students.

- ☛ What is there about this theme that makes it relevant to the children in my classroom?
- ☛ What opportunities for making connections between children and their world does this theme offer? Between what children know, want to know, and need to know? Between and among children?
- ☛ What makes me think that children would enjoy this theme?
- ☛ How does this theme allow for student choice and a range of interests, strengths, and abilities?
- ☛ Why is this theme a good use of my time and the children's time? Are there things of value to be learned by doing this theme?
- ☛ Are there real questions to be answered and is there a real audience for the "answers"?
- ☛ Does this theme give my children the opportunity to use a variety of learning processes?
- ☛ What curriculum content and processes does this theme address?

And the last and most important question, regardless of the theme, is

- ☛ When working on this theme, will my children feel secure, respected, cared for, appreciated, and supported in their learning?

**These are
our questions.**

What are yours?

As teachers we have had to make decisions about the ways in which we organize the learning in our classrooms. As our primary purpose in using themes has been to enhance learning, we developed these questions to guide our teaching practices based on what we believe about learners. By using these questions we increase our chances of being involved in themes that give children the opportunities to construct new knowledge, shape their attitudes, and increase their repertoire of skills and processes.

GETTING STARTED: SEEING THE POSSIBILITIES

Although many of you may already be using themes successfully in your classrooms, teachers always welcome new ideas. Here we provide some starting structures that can help you

- ☛ see possibilities for themes that arise from the kinds of events that take place in your classroom every day
- ☛ involve children in the planning stages
- ☛ custom-design themes to fit with you and the children in your classroom

You may also want to refer to chapter 7, page 58, where we note a number of themes that have been used with great success.

Getting Started: USING BOOKS TO BEGIN A THEME

The following is an example of how a book can be used to launch a theme or a number of concurrent themes.

1. The class read the story *The Paper Bag Princess* by Robert Munsch.

2. The teacher recorded the title of the book on a piece of chart paper and asked children the following questions:

   - ☛ Who is the author of this book?
   - ☛ Where does this story take place?
   - ☛ Who is the book about (main and supporting characters)?
   - ☛ What is this book about (big idea/theme)?
   - ☛ Is there anything else important about this book?

Preliminary web:
The Paper Bag Princess

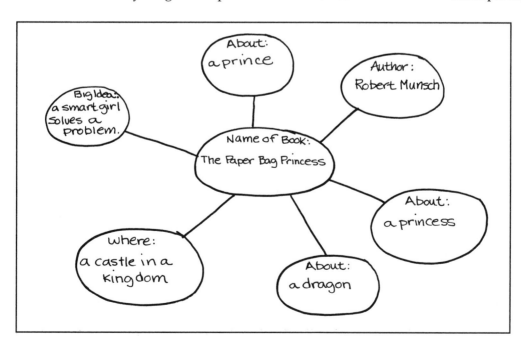

3. The teacher built upon the web by asking the following questions:

    Can you think of any other books/movies/television shows
    - ☞ written by this author?
    - ☞ about dragons?
    - ☞ that take place in castles and kingdoms?
    - ☞ about princesses?
    - ☞ about princes?
    - ☞ about girls that are strong and smart?

4. After the development of the web, children were asked to make a "one-sticker decision." The teacher handed one sticker to each child and invited small groups to come up to the web and place their stickers on the area that they would most like to have the opportunity to explore. The teacher said, "If you would like to read more books by Robert Munsch then place your sticker here. If you would like to read and study more about dragons then place your sticker here," and so on.

Detailed web:
The Paper Bag Princess

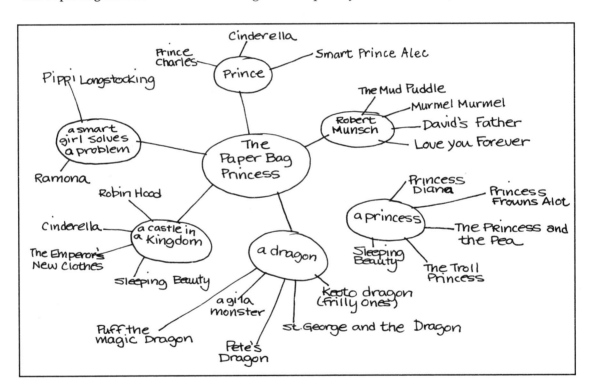

5. The part of the web that contained the most stickers became the next class theme. (An alternative to this would be to determine the three most popular items and then run three concurrent but complementary themes.)

Getting Started: USING OBJECTS BROUGHT IN BY CHILDREN

The following is an example of what can happen when a child brings an item to class that catches other children's interest. In this case the resulting theme was *Eggs*.

1. Doug brought the shell from a goose egg into the classroom to show the other children. The class listened intently as Doug explained where he had found it and what he thought it was.

2. The teacher capitalized on the children's obvious interest by putting the following headings on the chalkboard: What do you already know about eggs? What do you wonder about eggs? How can we find out answers to some of our questions?

3. Children volunteered their ideas and questions for each section as the teacher listed all responses on the board without question or comment, unless for clarification.

Chart about eggs

What do you already know about __eggs__ ?	What do you wonder about __eggs__ ?	How can we find out answers to some of our questions?
• they break • birds lay eggs • they crack • we eat them • at Easter we get chocolate eggs • we dye eggs for Easter • my mom scrambles eggs • dinosaurs laid eggs (big ones)	• how big do eggs get? • how does the bird get inside the egg? • how many kinds of eggs are there? • how do you make chocolate eggs with stuff inside them? • what kind of egg was Dougie's?	• books • my mom can make chocolate eggs • I watched a T.V. show on dinosaurs that told about their eggs

4. Following this session, the teacher sorted the children's questions into groups that focused on similar issues.

5. The teacher, with the help of the school librarian, gathered as many resource books, films, and videos as possible as a beginning for student investigations. She also asked children to bring any contributions they might have for the "egg table" in the classroom.

6. The teacher set up mixed-ability learning groups and invited five parents to come to the school that Friday, each to serve as a research assistant for one of the student groups.

7. The groups spent a good portion of Friday searching, sorting, and sharing, as well as exchanging information with other groups. The task in this collaborative activity was for each group to find out as much as it could to share with the whole class.

8. One way the groups shared information was through a picture display.

Picture display

Category	Research Assistant	Students	Our Drawings*		
What can eggs look like?	Mrs. Jacobs	Dawn Naoto Aaron Evelyn Danielle			
What kind of eggs do we eat?	Mrs. Harris	Shane Cody Emily Sam			
What size of eggs are there?	Mr. Duncan	Chelsea Leanne Shaun Pablo			
Where could eggs be found?	Mrs. Naidoo	Kelly Sheena Doug Ajmir			
What animals lay eggs?	Mrs. Zellinsky	Sally mark Jason Kelly. Kenzie			

*These drawings were done on Post-it Notes and placed on the grid by students as they found out new information.

Consider all the things your students might bring in that would spark a theme:

- fossils
- stamp collections
- rock tumbler
- newspaper article
- filmstrip
- news of a local protest
- news of an argument between students
- news of the death of a pet
- special book
- a student's baby picture
- news of the construction of a nearby building

- a bag of beautiful junk
- bird nest
- animal fur skin
- postcards from holiday
- photo album
- news of a community event
- provincial/state election comments
- news of the birth of a sibling
- a family "treasure"
- news of a playground incident
- news of a grandparent's visit
- a frog

Getting Started: USING ACTIVITY CENTERS TO KICK OFF A THEME

For those of us who have organized our classrooms into activity centers, the following example illustrates how something that happens in one center can be turned into a theme for the class, in this case a *Pirates* theme:

1. In activity-center time a small group of children took a piece of Styrofoam that had been part of some computer packing material and made a pirate ship. A few other children became interested in looking for materials to make more pirate ships.

2. When the teacher noticed the enthusiasm she asked, "What else do you need at the art center to build these ships?"

3. With the interested children she developed a list and posted it in the art center. The children collected all the materials that they could.

4. As even more children became interested in the topic of pirates, lists for other centers were developed.

5. Pirates "took over the room" at activity-center time. The teacher's major input had been helping children identify the materials they needed to continue. She supplied some; they supplied others.

> You are making pirate ships. What else would you like to have at the art center to use?
> - long sticks for masts
> - tape
> - more black paper
> - large white paper for the sails
> - pins for the railings
> - feathers
> - hooks

> Dramatic Play Center
> we need:
> - eye patches
> - swords
> - scarves
> - pirate pants
> - flags

Center signs

6. She continued to support the student learning by providing

- ☞ time for children to share their ideas and creations
- ☞ special books related to pirates that were read at book time (*The Man Whose Mother Was a Pirate* by Margaret Mahy was a class favorite.)
- ☞ opportunities for whole-class activities such as making treasure maps
- ☞ places to display their pirate creations

The study of pirates soon moved beyond activity-center time and became the thread for study in other subject areas. For example, some children did research on different types of boats, while others developed a script and produced their own pirate play.

Center signs

Library Center
we need:
- · skull and cross bone pictures
- · books of ships
- · maps
- · stories about pirates

Water and Sand Center
we need:
- · boats
- · lego people
- · pirate ships that float
- · treasure maps
- · buried treasure

Getting Started: MAKING CONNECTIONS WITH THE WORLD AROUND US

For all the children who love storybooks, there are just as many who are fascinated with books that deal with the world of nature. The following activity, which started out as a *Frogs* theme and developed into an *Animals* theme, gave children an opportunity to connect fact and fantasy and broadened the horizons of all.

1. The class had some tadpoles in the room as part of their science unit.

2. The teacher read *Frog and Toad* by Arnold Lobel. As they talked about it together, the children started to talk about what they knew about their real tadpoles and the things that the frogs in the book could do. They were trying to figure out why some frogs were different.

3. The teacher made the following grid on the board and worked with the children as they generated ideas to fit under each heading:

Real Frogs	Frogs in Storybooks
• are usually green • have tails when they are babies • live in the water and on the land • eat bugs	• talk • have friends • are like us • wear clothes • can disappear and become princes • have houses

Chart about frogs

4. The teacher went to the library with the children, who collected every book (fiction and nonfiction) that they could find—whether they could read it or not—that had a frog in it. They came back to their classroom loaded down with books and spent time reading, looking at pictures, and just browsing.

5. The process continued each time the teacher or one of the children read a book. Each time someone made a discovery everyone would stop, and the discovery would be recorded on the grid.

6. After two weeks spent adding to this grid, each student made a poster showing either a real frog or a storybook frog that had caught his or her interest.

7. As the interest in doing comparisons was still high, the children brainstormed all the animals that they had read about in storybooks as the teacher recorded this list on the chalkboard. Children printed their initials on the board by their favorite animal. Those children who chose the same animal ended up working together, while others worked on their own.

8. The class went to the library to hunt for books about the animals they had selected. The children created comparison charts for each animal and represented what they had learned about their animals in a variety of ways, from a plasticine mouse to a diorama of a lion's den.

Getting Started: USING OTHER PEOPLE'S COLLECTIONS

Parents and other community members have much to share—collections, expertise, and stories. Here is one example of a class that learned through interaction with someone outside their class as they focused on a *Northern Canada* theme.

1. One parent brought her collection of artifacts from the Canadian North.

2. She left the collection on display with the class for one day under the teacher's supervision.

3. During free time, the students each made a list of three "notice thats…" that they had observed about the collection.

4. After the class discussed different types of interview questions beyond ones requiring simple yes-or-no answers, each student was given a piece of paper with a large X dividing the page. All the children then wrote four questions on their sheets that they wanted to ask the owner of the collection.

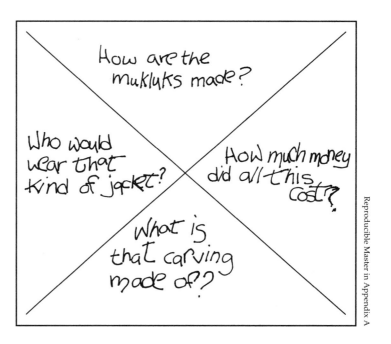

Cross-examination form

Reproducible Master in Appendix A

5. To help practice their interview techniques, the children questioned each other, alternatively taking on the role of the expert and of the questioner.

6. The owner of the collection made a second visit to the classroom, and children, in groups of three, got to "cross-examine" the guest for five minutes while the others observed and made notes.

7. Following the cross-examinations, all students wrote down three things they had learned, how they felt about what they had learned, and what they wanted to find out more about.

Getting Started: USING SCHOOL EVENTS

Our classes are often invited to whole-school events that have little apparent connection to what is going on in our classrooms. The following is an example of one way to capitalize on the opportunity that these occasions present. In this case, attending a band performance led to a *Musical Instruments* theme.

1. The class went to the gym to hear a local school band play. When the class returned to its room, children were talking about the "big kids," the different instruments, and the songs.

2. When the teacher noticed that the class had so much to say about the performance, he went to the chalkboard and wrote the heading, "Our Questions." As the teacher recorded them on the board, children asked all the questions they could think of.

3. The next day the teacher looked at the list and told the class that he didn't know the answer to a lot of the questions. He put a new heading on the board, "How Can We Find Out?" and, along with the class, he contributed different ways that they could find out some answers to their questions.

"Our Questions" list; "How Can We Find Out?" list

4. The teacher suggested to the children that for one week they search for answers to their questions. They decided that for

Our Questions
- What was the big instrument with the loudest noise?
- How can I be in the band?
- What does the drum set cost?
- What is the most expensive instrument?
- Which is the hardest instrument to play?
- Which is the easiest to play?
- Why do they only have one set of drums?
- What do the conductors' signals mean?
- How much do they have to practice?
- Do they go on trips?
- What's a marching band?
- How much does the big, huge horn weigh?

How Can We Find out?
- go to the library
- ask someone
  - our music teacher
  - Andrea, because she takes music lessons
  - my dad, because he plays the trumpet
- bring instruments to class
- ask the high school kids to come back
- call the principal at the high school
- the high school music teacher
- books from home
- films, videos, television

each of the first four days of the week they would refer to a different source.

- ☞ Monday—Invite our music teacher into class
- ☞ Tuesday—Watch a video called *The Instruments*
- ☞ Wednesday—Bring a piece of information or an instrument from home
- ☞ Thursday—Invite two high-school students who are in the band to class for interviews

On Friday the teacher prepared a list of possible ways to represent what the children had learned during the week.

> Ways we can show what we know
>
> singing   painting   reports
> talking   making models
> drawing   posters   writing
> dioramas   acting   letters

"Ways we can show what we know"

Getting Started: USING A SUBJECT AREA

Sometimes a class shows special interest in a particular area. In one class the children were obviously interested in numbers and things to do with mathematics. The teacher suggested to the children that they could do a theme all about math.

1. They recorded all the ways they used math in their classroom.

2. After the students discussed all the ways they used math at school, the teacher asked them to think about the ways they used math at home. Each child became a Math Detective and all the detectives collected examples of how math was used at home.

3. The class then developed a list of math words and questions.

4. The class made an inventory of all the materials in the math center and then searched out and/or made new math games and materials.

5. The teacher used the children's interest to introduce activities that became part of the children's weekly routine. These activities included Mystery Numbers, Riddles, Estimations of Objects in a Container, and Collecting Statistics About Our World. They began to collect a million bread tags and enlisted school-wide support. This meant that each day they needed to calculate and recalculate the total collected. They also wrote regular reports for the school newsletter.

A math web

6. Other activities arose from student interest (and from students' annoyances with certain practices). As information could help influence decision-making, the students decided to conduct a school-wide environment survey to determine if the school's environmental awareness and recycling program was effective. Some students decided to keep statistics of the use of the playing fields by different ages of students, while another group decided to record the number of children wearing bike helmets that they observed over a one-week period. Information about the many student projects was recorded on a wall chart, and any new questions generated were added to the question board. This collection of "raw data" became the basis for letters that were written and sent, as well as presentations made to the school principal and students in other classrooms.

Getting Started: USING A PROCESS

To help her class learn how to respond to text in a variety of ways, one teacher explained that the students would be learning a variety of strategies to help them think about the stories they were reading.

1. To begin the theme, students talked about books that had captured their imaginations, and then selected one of these.

2. The teacher then read a chapter of the chosen book aloud and asked the students how readers could find out more about the story or share what they knew, listing the strategies on the chalkboard that the children told her they used when reading.

3. The teacher explained that at a recent conference she had learned some new ways to respond to text and had a number of books that explained many more. Putting the children in groups, she enlisted the students' help to try out the various new strategies suggested, record those that worked best for them, and then "teach" those strategies to the other students. Each group was to look for one strategy that it liked and thought other students would enjoy. For example, one group chose a prediction strategy, while another elected to do a story map. (See *Literacy Through Literature* by Terry Johnson and Daphne Louis.)

4. Using a collection of professional books with some of the more straightforward strategies highlighted, the children worked in their groups to figure out what the author was suggesting, then tried out each strategy using one of the books that they had already read. Some of the professional texts they used included *Literacy Through Literature*, *Reaching for Higher Thought*, *Bringing It All Together*, and *Creating Classrooms for Authors* (see Suggested Reading, page 77).

5. The strategies used by the groups were listed on the chalkboard. Over the next couple of weeks the whole class was introduced to each strategy by the teacher, with the student "strategy experts" helping. As the students tried activities such as making story maps, they talked about how these techniques could help them solve problems when they were reading or organize their ideas.

6. When the students had built up a bank of strategies, they worked with partners to develop independence in using these strategies. They kept lists of the strategies they could use and a list of books that they had used them with.

The time invested in this learning process was an investment that produced long-term returns. By going through a process together to learn about reader response, thinking, writing, or representing, the students developed awareness, a class vocabulary, and a range of strategies they can apply in other learning situations.

Getting Started: USING A BIG ISSUE

One major issue that affects all of us is the environment. One teacher, wanting to provide an opportunity for children to pursue issues they had indicated as being of concern and interest, decided to pose three questions to the class:

- ☞ Why would learning about the environment be a good use of our time?
- ☞ What can children do that makes a difference?
- ☞ What can we all do to make a difference?

The search for answers became the focus of activity for several weeks and provided ongoing interest for the school year. One guide established by the teacher was that the students' work must focus on *showing* what they could do rather than *telling* what they might do. Other teachers and classes of students in the school became involved.

Some of the resulting projects included

- ☞ posters that showed the number of flattened juice boxes collected in one week of school lunches
- ☞ letters to manufacturers requesting recyclable containers
- ☞ raising money to purchase acres of rain forest by growing and selling bedding plants for flower boxes
- ☞ planting trees on the playground that particularly suited that habitat
- ☞ making recycling boxes for each classroom and working with adults to develop a workable collection process
- ☞ working with a local gardener to learn how to design and build a compost bin and sharing that information with parents in a school newsletter
- ☞ working with a carpenter to build birdhouses to attract birds that are in danger of losing their habitat
- ☞ building an outhouse for a local nature park
- ☞ seeding the local oyster beds

This theme was successful because the children were actively engaged in demonstrating their solutions. The need to *show*, not just *tell*, made this theme come alive and helped students realize the value of their efforts.

What are some possibilities you could use as theme starters?

In this chapter we've given some examples of successful theme starters. Because each classroom is unique, there can be as many possibilities for starting themes as there are children and teachers to create them.

KEEPING ON COURSE—USING PLANNING CHARTS

In the last chapter we gave some examples of the ways in which themes can get started. Whether they are effective or not depends on the relevance and appeal that they have for you and for your children.

The most successful technique we know of to plan well-balanced, curriculum-connected theme experiences is to use planning charts similar to the ones displayed on the opposite page.

EVOLUTION OF A THEME

The starter for the theme about money was a visit from a parent who had just received an award for the design of one of the new (1992) Canadian quarters. The purpose of her visit was to show the

children some steps in the design process and tell them about her work. During her visit it was obvious that the children were keenly interested in what she had to say and that the whole topic of money was fascinating to them. Realizing this, the teacher did some preliminary planning before talking to the class about the possibilities of extending their interest into a theme. (See teacher's preliminary web, opposite page.)

When the teacher looked at her web she felt there was enough substance in the theme to make it worthwhile. She decided to put forth the topic of money as a suggestion to the class.

When the teacher met with her class she said, "I felt you were really interested in money when Mrs. E. visited. Would you like to do some more on this topic?" She was greeted with many enthusiastic "yes" responses. She then asked the class what they could do to learn about money. The children made the suggestions shown in the web on page 22.

As the theme evolved, the children visited a bank and represented their experience through their classroom bank and by making dioramas of the bank. The class store they set up is still flourishing, and an unexpected learning opportunity came about when the class had a used toy sale to raise money for a local Christmas fund. They also broadened their knowledge of money and

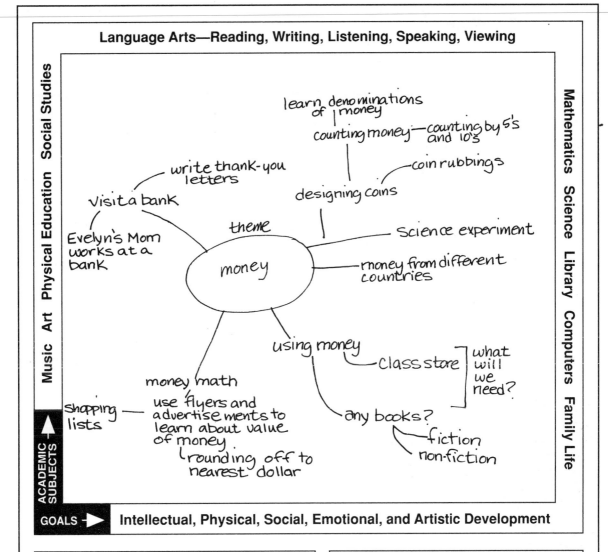

Language Arts—Reading, Writing, Listening, Speaking, Viewing

Social Studies · *Physical Education* · *Art* · *Music*

Mathematics Science Library Computers Family Life

ACADEMIC SUBJECTS →

GOALS → **Intellectual, Physical, Social, Emotional, and Artistic Development**

Within the web:

learn denominations of money

counting money — counting by 5's and 10's

coin rubbings

designing coins

write thank-you letters

Visit a bank

Evelyn's Mom works at a bank

theme

money

science experiment

money from different countries

using money

Class store — what will we need?

any books? — fiction, non-fiction

money math

use flyers and advertisements to learn about value of money

shopping lists

rounding off to nearest dollar

TEACHER REFLECTIONS

This theme has possibilities because…
- the kids seemed so keen and enthusiasm is obvious
- it fits in with math curriculum
- it connects to Social Studies (store, bank, money from other countries)
- we could do a potato experiment to show how dirty money is
- we could look at designs on coins and bills and design our own rubbings
- great potential for drama!
- Language Arts?? Physical Education? not much but the kids are "cooking" with their own reading and writing projects now and P.E. doesn't have to fit!

GUIDE QUESTIONS

- Is this theme relevant to children?
- Are there opportunities for connections?
- Will it generate enthusiasm/enjoyment?
- Does it allow for student choice and a range of interests, abilities, and strengths?
- Is it a good use of our time?
- Are there real questions to be answered and a real audience for the answers?
- Does it give children the opportunity to use a variety of learning processes?
- What curriculum content and processes does this theme address?

Teacher's preliminary web

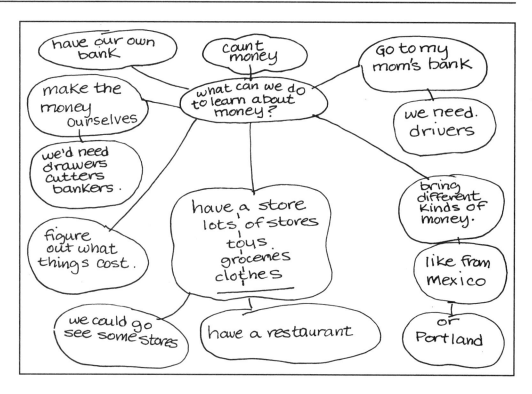

Students' web   stores by using the money they raised to shop for gifts for the Christmas hamper. From a curriculum perspective the theme was successful in helping the children build and extend concepts in math and social studies. It gave them opportunities to cooperate and collaborate as well as use language skills (for example, working in the store and bank, making lists, planning, interviewing, and writing letters).

Although the theme "officially ended" when the school closed for the holidays, the children's continuing interest in money makes itself obvious through the comments the children make and the skills they display as they are involved in other activities.

To define and organize her students' learning experiences, one teacher made the web about inventions (see opposite page) based on her own planning and discussions with her students.

To try out the match between the *Oceans* study and cultural studies (social studies), the teacher made curriculum connections in "mind map" form (see page 24). While some teachers might do this as a checklist, many teachers find that "mind mapping" lends itself more easily to showing the interconnections between curriculum areas.

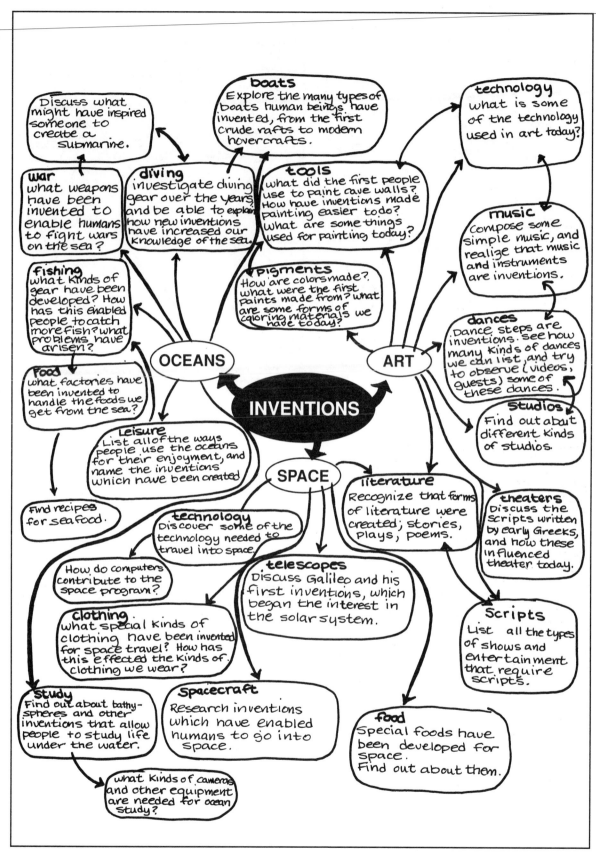

boats
Explore the many types of boats human beings have invented, from the first crude rafts to modern hovercrafts.

technology
What is some of the technology used in art today?

Discuss what might have inspired someone to create a submarine.

diving
investigate diving gear over the years, and be able to explain how new inventions have increased our knowledge of the sea.

tools
What did the first people use to paint cave walls? How have inventions made painting easier to do? What are some things used for painting today?

war
What weapons have been invented to enable humans to fight wars on the sea?

music
Compose some simple music, and realize that music and instruments are inventions.

fishing
What kinds of gear have been developed? How has this enabled people to catch more fish? What problems have arisen?

pigments
How are colors made? What were the first paints made from? What are some forms of coloring materials we have today?

dances
Dance steps are inventions. See how many kinds of dances we can list, and try to observe (videos, guests) some of these dances.

food
What factories have been invented to handle the foods we get from the sea?

OCEANS

ART

INVENTIONS

studios
Find out about different kinds of studios.

Leisure
List all of the ways people use the oceans for their enjoyment, and name the inventions which have been created

Find recipes for seafood.

SPACE

literature
Recognize that forms of literature were created; stories, plays, poems.

theaters
Discuss the scripts written by early Greeks, and how these influenced theater today.

technology
Discover some of the technology needed to travel into space.

How do computers contribute to the space program?

telescopes
Discuss Galileo and his first inventions, which began the interest in the solar system.

Scripts
List all the types of shows and entertainment that require scripts.

clothing
What special kinds of clothing have been invented for space travel? How has this effected the kinds of clothing we wear?

study
Find out about bathyspheres and other inventions that allow people to study life under the water.

Spacecraft
Research inventions which have enabled humans to go into space.

food
Special foods have been developed for space. Find out about them.

What kinds of cameras and other equipment are needed for ocean study?

A web on Inventions *theme*

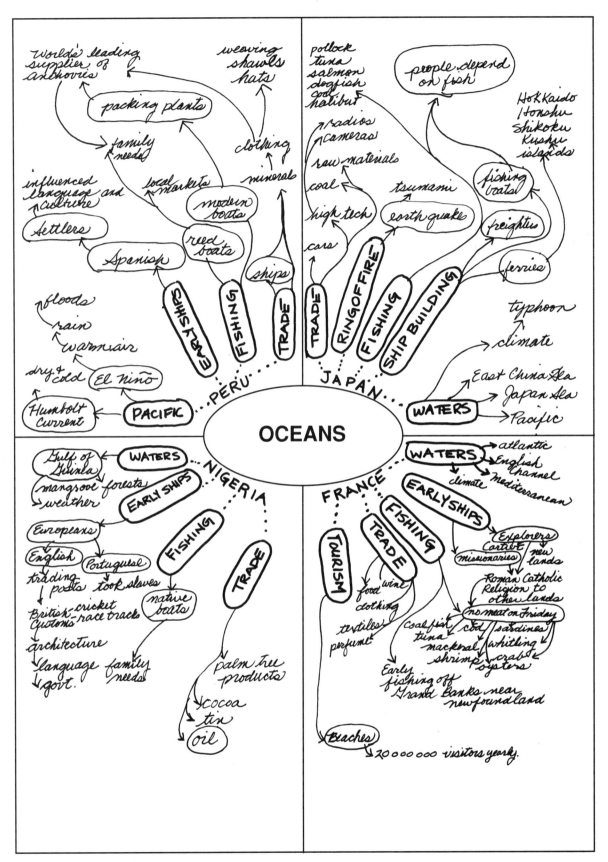

Oceans *mind map*

Each theme provides many opportunities to read about, write about, listen to, talk about, and represent what we know. Themes bring meaningful reasons for doing and learning into our classrooms. As teachers, we use themes to increase students' opportunities for learning. The processes that teachers choose to highlight during the course of a theme depends on their students' learning needs. Planning for a theme has less to do with creating excitement—although successful themes are usually exciting for all involved—than with providing ways for children to practice and improve in "the basics"—and demanding that they think critically and learn how to learn.

In chapter 5, we provide many suggestions for ways to conclude themes and acknowledge the learning that has occurred. We hope that you will select from the variety of beginnings and endings we have suggested, and mix, match, and extend them to suit your needs and those of your students.

What kinds of planning strategies work for you and your students?

4

ASSESSING AND EVALUATING—HOW DO WE KNOW OUR CHILDREN ARE LEARNING?

We discuss assessment at this point in the book, as we believe it is important to ensure that learning is taking place while work on a theme is *still in progress*. In this way there is time to make any necessary adjustments to the plans.

As the primary value of using a theme approach is in the real learning that takes place, our assessment and evaluation in any theme must focus on that learning. Assessment involves gathering the evidence of what children have done or can do. Evaluation involves interpreting the evidence in light of our goals and expectations for learning within each theme.

As teachers, we routinely assess and evaluate what takes place in our classrooms as we are accountable for what we teach children. We assess and evaluate what is working and what is not working for students as a planning necessity—as a basis of knowledge for making future plans and for making adjustments to a plan in progress. We also assess and evaluate what is going on in our classrooms to determine if our practices are congruent with what we know about how children learn.

As teachers, we have all developed ways of organizing and recording what is taking place in the classroom. The following frames have proved to be effective in the assessment and evaluation of themes.

CONNECTING TO THE CURRICULUM

We believe that organizing our teaching around themes helps us to make the best use of children's time and offers them a rich spectrum of learning opportunities. But is important to be able to link the exciting activities in which our children are engaged to the curriculum requirements in our particular area, to assess whether or not the curricular goals are being met.

Language Arts Skills Month April

Skills and Processes	Week of 8-12	Week of 15-19	Week of 22-26	Week of 29-30
contractions	I			
root words	I			
prefixes (un, re, dis, im, in, pre)	I			
suffixes (ful, ness, y, ly, tion)	I			
dictionary guide words	W			
multiple meanings				
plurals				
possessives	G			

Skills taught in the context of student work
I means you work with an individual or individuals/ maybe in a conference as you talk with them about their writing

W is a whole class activity
G is for a group of children that you brought together for the same skill

"Curriculum Connections" form

OBSERVING AND RECORDING CHILDREN'S LEARNING

If we are going to be able to assess progress, we need to collect and record evidence of children's learning during each theme. Teachers have their own systems for observing and recording children's learning. The samples on page 28 are two simple methods that have worked for us.

ALIGNING OUR PRACTICE WITH WHAT WE KNOW ABOUT LEARNING (ASSESSMENT)

The same questions we asked ourselves in chapter 2, "Deciding on a Theme—Looking Ahead," can be adapted to help us reflect on the worth of a theme under way. Using these questions helps us to see whether or not the plans we've made and the experiences in which we've engaged children meet our criteria for effective learning.

☞ Is this theme relevant to the children in my classroom?

Assessing and Evaluating—How Do We Know Our Children Are Learning? 27

Observations Being Made				
Name	working with others	use of resource materials		
Naoto	helped Chad w/o taking over Nov 18			
Aaron				
Emily		brought atlas from home Oct. 12		
Wey Ming				
Sean				

Theme	Naoto	Aaron	Emily	Danielle	chelsea	Leanne	shaun
Space							
Focus	Shane	Evelyn	Cody	Shanda	Pablo	Dawn	Wey Ming
How are children using problem solving strategies?	Mark	Leon	Sheena	Kenzie	Sam	Ajmir	Doug
	Jason	Kelly	Sally	Ramon	Nancy	Keoko	
Date							

Two methods of observing and recording children's learning

- What kinds of connections am I observing? Between the children and their world? Between what they knew, wanted to know, and needed to know? Between and among themselves?
- What shows me and/or tells me that this theme is enjoyable for these children?
- How does this theme allow for student choice and a range of interests, strengths, and abilities? How can I make it meet these needs more effectively?
- Why is this theme a good use of my time and the children's time? What is being learned that is of value?
- What real questions are being pursued and what real audiences do my children have for their work?
- What processes are my children using and learning during this theme?
- What curriculum content and processes is this theme addressing?
- What evidence do I have that my children feel secure, respected, cared for, appreciated, and supported in their learning?

ALIGNING OUR PRACTICE WITH WHAT WE KNOW ABOUT LEARNING (EVALUATION)

The same kinds of questions we asked ourselves on page 6, "Deciding on a Theme—Looking Ahead," and above (assessment) can be adapted to be equally effective in helping us reflect on the worth of a theme under way or a theme that has just been completed. Using these questions helps us see whether or not the plans we've made and the experiences in which we've engaged the children meet our criteria for effective learning.

- How was this theme relevant to the children in my classroom?
- What kinds of connections did I observe? Between the children and their world? Between what they knew, wanted to know, and needed to know? Between and among themselves?
- What showed me and/or told me that this theme was enjoyable for these children?
- How did this theme allow for student choice and a range of interests, strengths, and abilities?
- Why was this theme a good use of my time and the children's time? What was learned that is of value?
- What real questions were answered, and what real audiences did my children find?

What assessment and evaluation strategies work for you and your children?

- What processes did my children use and learn during this theme?
- What curriculum content and processes did this theme address?
- What evidence do I have that my children felt secure, respected, cared for, appreciated, and supported in their learning?

INVOLVING CHILDREN IN THE EVALUATION PROCESS

As a result of what we know about how children learn, we are committed to including children in the evaluation process. Through self-evaluation children

- find out what they know
- inform their teacher and parents about their learning
- develop pride in their efforts and accomplishments
- set new learning goals

There are many ways that children can collect and organize information about their own learning. Their self-evaluation can be as

simple as a sheet of paper saying, "During our theme on _____ I learned _____ _____ and _____ ,"

or as comprehensive as a personal collection/ portfolio.

You could use or adapt the examples on the following pages to help your children evaluate their learning experiences.

To show what I know about _____
(theme)

I _____
(made a model, wrote a poem, drew a picture…)

Three things I want you to notice are

•

•

•

Name _____

Theme _____

Three things my friends would say that they learned from me when we studied

_____
(theme)

are…

•

•

•

Name _____

Theme _____

Three things that I learned from my friends when we studied

_____
(theme)

are…

•

•

•

One thing I learned today

about _____
(theme)

that I could teach someone

at home is _____

_____

_____

_____

Dear _____ ,
(teacher)

If you do this theme on _____
with another class I would suggest that you could
make it better by

1.

2.

3.

The other thing I'd like to tell you is _____

_____

signed _____

Date _____ Theme _____

Here is a photo of me working

with _____

(place photo here)

When we work together we can _____

_____

All children need frequent opportunities for oral
rehearsal—opportunities to self-evaluate *orally
first*—to be able to move beyond trite responses.

☆ For younger children these are done orally
and the frames may be used as oral prompts.

*Frames for children's
self-evaluation*

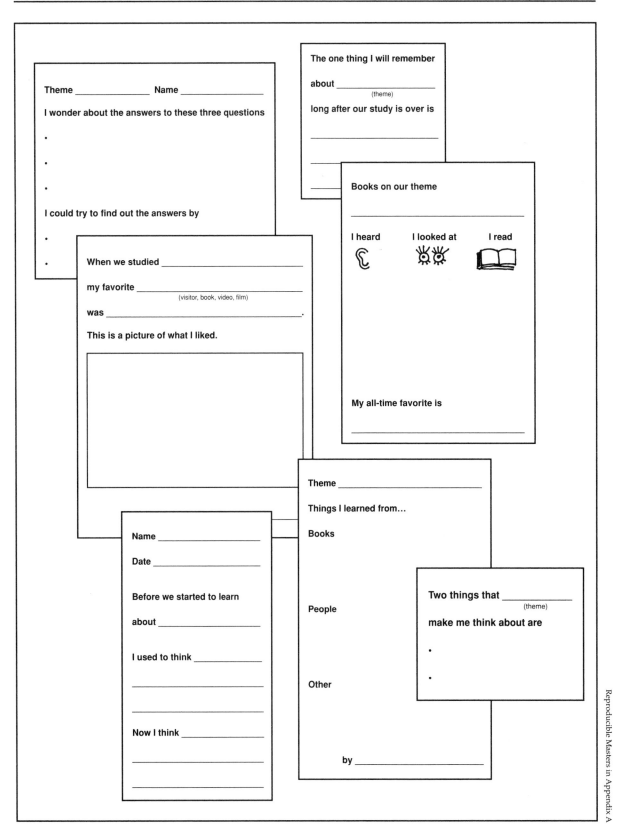

Theme _____ Name _____

I wonder about the answers to these three questions

•

•

•

I could try to find out the answers by

•

•

The one thing I will remember

about _____
(theme)

long after our study is over is

_____

When we studied _____

my favorite _____
(visitor, book, video, film)

was _____.

This is a picture of what I liked.

Books on our theme

_____

I heard   I looked at   I read

My all-time favorite is

_____

Name _____

Date _____

Before we started to learn

about _____

I used to think _____

_____

_____

Now I think _____

_____

_____

Theme _____

Things I learned from...

Books

People

Other

by _____

Two things that _____
(theme)

make me think about are

•

•

*Frames for children's
self-evaluation*

THEME PORTFOLIOS

A theme portfolio is an effective way to demonstrate the scope of children's learning and development. As the theme progresses, children place carefully chosen examples of their representations, or comments on their learning, in individual file folders. These will later be shared with their parents. Teachers can give guidance by suggesting a criterion to children, such as a piece the child is proud of, a piece a child would like to work on again, or a piece that shows the child was really thinking. The index below is one example of what such a portfolio might contain.

THEME PORTFOLIO INDEX

• A list of books that I have looked at, heard, or read.
• My burning questions
• A photograph of our group at work.
• something I made when studying this theme that I'd like to have the chance to do again
• a letter of advice to my teacher.
• other

Reproducible Master in Appendix A

5

TELLING, SHOWING, AND CELEBRATING WHAT WE KNOW

The time to end a theme becomes apparent when we have accomplished what we and our children agreed to do, when we have run out of resources, or more frequently, when our students' interest in a particular topic has waned. The appropriate time to end a theme is not when we have completed a certain number of activities, but when the theme's ability to inspire learning has run its course. However much time we have spent on a theme, or whatever the breadth and depth of our discoveries and involvement, there comes a time when an official tying together is necessary.

The possibilities for theme endings that we suggest in the following section will help children and teachers identify and appreciate what has been accomplished. This is done by highlighting the processes, skills, and knowledge that have been expanded upon or introduced, and by providing opportunities to share and celebrate learning.

Of course some children may maintain an active interest in topics that have been especially relevant to them. One benefit of using themes is that we give children opportunities to discover and display their individual interests and abilities. With each theme we can

help children acknowledge particular fascination with, or expertise in, certain areas. (Is there a teacher anywhere who hasn't met at least one child whose knowledge of dinosaurs rivals that of the curator of the local museum?) As we recognize the personal connections that children make and help them connect their understanding in one area to new topics, we identify the threads that become the fabric of our classroom tapestry.

Before we can know what knowledge or skills children are acquiring, they must be able to communicate their thinking in some way. The greater the variety of representations that we encourage, the more opportunities we give children to develop their unique strengths and abilities.

ENDING A THEME: TELLING WHAT WE KNOW

One way that children can communicate what they know is by verbally presenting what they have learned to an audience. Audiences can include school administrators, big buddies, parents, other classes, senior citizens, local media, support staff in the school, and school board officials and trustees. We and our students can choose how to present orally what has been learned during a theme. Oral presentations may take many forms. Some suggestions included in this chapter are: a one-minute speech on a topic; acrostic poetry; class meetings; a countdown of ten top points; the activities Two, Four, Maybe More, Ping-Pong, Summary Circle, and Old Questions, New Questions, Burning Questions. As we end a theme, we work with children to select the most appropriate audience for our learning as well as the most effective form of presentation. Essentially we mix and match audiences and presentation formats to create the best endings for any particular theme.

Talk as representation of learning

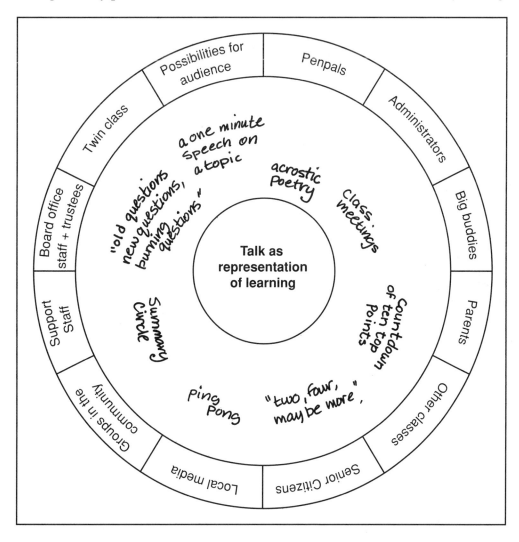

Here are three of our favorite ways to use talk as an effective way for children to share their learning and for us to conclude a theme.

Telling what we know: PING-PONG

This activity is particularly useful for bringing out different aspects of a theme. For example, when finishing a theme about places where people live, the teacher used the following plan.

1. The class was divided into two groups.

2. One group was responsible for making a list of "city" words, and the other made a list of "country" words. Each group printed its words on separate cards, which were distributed to its members until all students had at least one card.

3. Holding their word cards, the children lined up on opposite sides of the room. The teacher acted as the moderator saying, while pointing to the first student on the "country" side, "The country has..." The student responded, "Fresh air!" The teacher then turned and said, "The city has..." The first child on the "city" side replied, "Tall buildings!" This pattern was repeated until everyone had had at least one turn.

After modeling this process once, teachers can ask a student to act as a moderator for the activity. When children become more comfortable with the game, they are able to respond spontaneously, without relying on their printed cards.

Telling what we know: OLD QUESTIONS, NEW QUESTIONS, BURNING QUESTIONS

When a theme has begun with children's questions, this activity provides a suitable closure.

1. On the chalkboard, record the class's original questions about a particular theme. Supply each child with a copy of this list of questions. Then have children, using highlighters, mark those questions that were answered during the theme.

2. The teacher then asks, "Did we find the answers to all our questions?" recording the group's consensus on the original chart. If there are questions that remain unanswered, the class may decide what action, if any, it wants to take. A further step, if children are interested, could be to ask, "Do you have additional questions to ask now?" These new questions could then be recorded on the chart or on the chalkboard.

3. After steps 1 and 2, the teacher asks, "Do you really want to find more out about any of these questions?" Children write

their responses in a small class-made book entitled "Burning Questions." The teacher then allocates time on a regular basis to talk about the students' progress in answering their unanswered original questions or subsequent new questions.

Telling what we know: TWO, FOUR, MAYBE MORE

This is an activity that encourages children to tell others what they have learned. Through the telling, children become better prepared to share their learning with their parents and others.

1. Each child finds a partner (teachers can encourage children to work with others by asking them to select a partner based on, for example, birthdays in the same month, similar styles of track shoes, or the same first initials of their last names). The partners then tell each other two things that they learned during the course of the theme and one thing that they would still like to know more about.

2. Each pair then joins with another pair and they share what they have learned with each other.

3. The groups keep expanding, and sharing what they have learned, until the class has merged into two large groups. In this way, the children have the opportunity to "tell what they know."

ENDING A THEME: SHOWING WHAT WE KNOW

Another way that children can share what they know is by showing an audience what they have learned. When we and our students choose how to represent what has been learned, we consider individual preferences and material to be presented and then make a match. We may choose, for example, to make a banner, conduct a survey, create a word search, produce a slide show, draw cartoons, write a book, or create a model.

The examples that follow are three successful ways of using child-made products to provide us with insights into students' learning. At the same time each acts as a vehicle for concluding a theme.

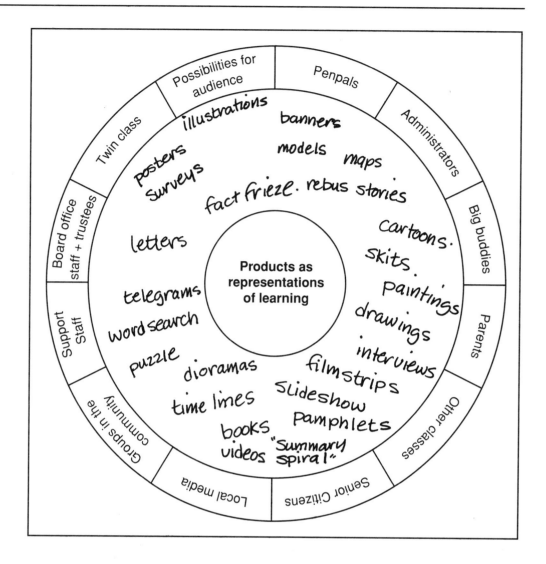

Outer ring labels (clockwise from top): Possibilities for audience · Penpals · Administrators · Big buddies · Parents · Other classes · Senior Citizens · Local media · Groups in the community · Support Staff · Board office staff + trustees · Twin class

Inner labels: Products as representations of learning

illustrations · banners · models · maps · posters · surveys · fact frieze · rebus stories · cartoons · skits · paintings · letters · drawings · telegrams · interviews · word search · filmstrips · puzzle · dioramas · Slideshow · time lines · Pamphlets · books · videos · "Summary Spiral"

Products as representations of learning

Showing what we know: SUMMARY SPIRAL

The interesting design of this format provides children with a way to summarize their learning on a theme or topic. The shape can also vary so as to represent some key aspect of the theme. For example, following a theme focused on sea life the information might take the shape of fish.

After children have completed their spirals, they can exchange with other students to share their learning or do some mutual editing. Published copies of these spirals are excellent ways to show parents what children are learning.

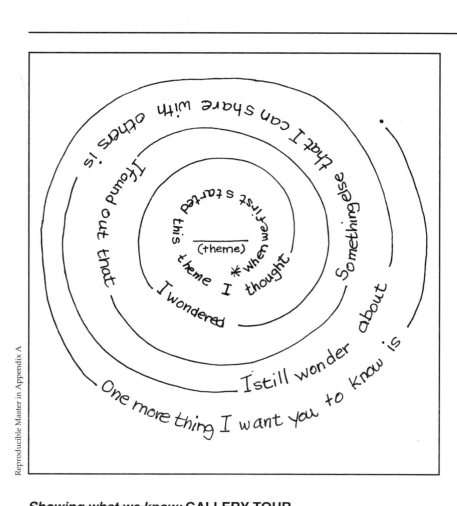

Reproducible Master in Appendix A

Spiral text (reading from center outward):

(theme)

* when we first started
this theme I thought

I wondered

I found out that

Something else that I can share with others is

I still wonder about

One more thing I want you to know is

Summary spiral

Showing what we know: GALLERY TOUR

When children have created products such as models, structures, dioramas, or plasticine figurines, these can be displayed with some information about the creators.

1. Display children's creations around the classroom in art gallery style using countertops or tables.

2. Before beginning their tours of the work displayed, have each child randomly select a card with another child's name printed on it to use as a "compliment card." After viewing all the work exhibited, each child fills out the compliment card for his or her classmate and also thinks of at least one comment about the work in general.

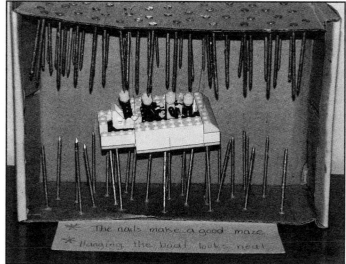

```
┌─────────────────────────────────────────────────┐
│  COMPLIMENT CARD FOR _____      │
│                                                   │
│  ☆                                                │
│                                                   │
│                                                   │
│  ☆                                                │
│                                                   │
└─────────────────────────────────────────────────┘
```

Compliment card

3. The children then meet as a group and share their impressions of the exhibits. Giving compliments takes practice. A frame such as, "One thing that impressed me about all of our work was…" will help them be specific and positive.

4. To share individual compliments each child must find the person whose name he or she selected and read the card. (Chaotic but worthwhile!)

Showing what we know: FACT FRIEZE

As an alternative to writing, a fact frieze provides children with a way to display their knowledge about a particular theme.

1. The teacher records a list of the children's "most important facts" about a theme that they have been studying.

2. Each child chooses a partner and selects one of the facts to illustrate. The teacher provides all the pairs of children with the same size sheets of rectangular paper on which to create their pictures. To determine whether their representations are accurate, children double-check their facts with the resource materials they have been using.

3. If more industrious partners finish sooner than the others, give them the option of reviewing the list and selecting another fact to "freeze."

4. The teacher and children arrange the drawings in a connected linear display—a frieze.

5. Besides enjoying this display themselves, students may choose to exchange friezes with their "big buddies" in the school or with a class of pen pals.

Our Most Important Facts About Birds
   * there many different Kinds of birds
   * most birds can fly
   * birds have feathers

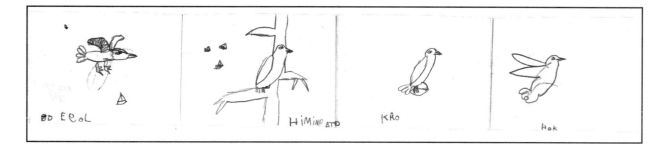

BD EPoL   HiMiNO BTD   KRo   Hok

ENDING A THEME: CELEBRATING WHAT WE KNOW

Fact frieze

Learning is more likely to be retained if it is connected to pleasurable experiences. Although opportunities for children to have fun occur throughout the course of a theme, one of our favorite ways to end a theme is by having some kind of celebration that gives children the opportunity to share their learning. Celebrations can include a per-

formance of some kind, a return to a starting event (such as a former field trip destination), an open house, or a demonstration. The celebration you select needs to be matched with an appropriate audience—sometimes including other classes, school buddies, parents, senior citizens, or local media. Teachers must determine the best way for children to share what they have learned during the course of a theme.

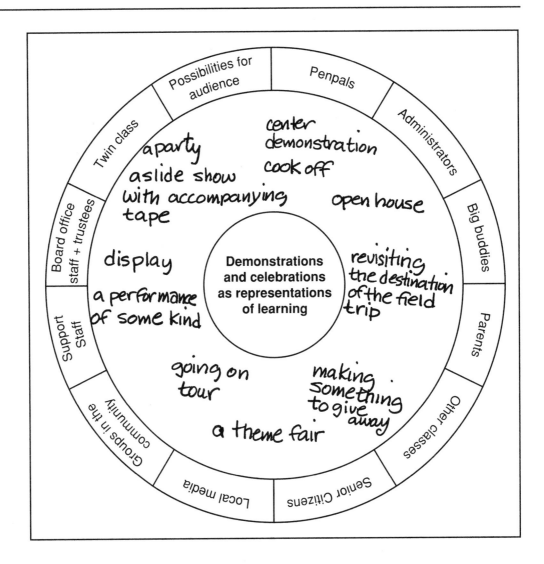

Inside the wheel (clockwise from top):
Possibilities for audience — Penpals — Administrators — Big buddies — Parents — Other classes — Senior Citizens — Local media — Groups in the community — Support Staff — Board office staff + trustees — Twin class

Center circle: **Demonstrations and celebrations as representations of learning**

Surrounding text:
a party
a slide show with accompanying tape
display
a performance of some kind
center demonstration
cook off
open house
revisiting the destination of the field trip
going on tour
making something to give away
a theme fair

Demonstrations and celebrations as representations of learning

Celebrating what we know: THEME FAIR

Organizing a fair is a great way to end a theme. The example that follows is how one class set up a fair at the conclusion of its *Safety* theme, although other highly successful fairs have been arranged around such topics as awareness of the people with special needs, multiculturalism, the environment, and fitness.

1. The students wrote to people responsible for safety programs in their community, for example, the fire chief, police captain, hydro-electric supervisor, search-and-rescue coordinator, and the director of earthquake preparedness. They asked them if their agencies would set up and supervise displays in the school gymnasium on the afternoon and evening of the fair.

2. The teacher and volunteer parents confirmed dates and attendance with each agency. They helped children arrange for appropriate display areas.

3. The children wrote invitations to their parents and made posters and advertisements to invite other classes and community members.

4. The teacher helped the children make a sign-up schedule for other classes.

5. On the day of the safety fair, the students worked in pairs to act as hosts for the exhibitors and to conduct guided tours of the display area.

6. Following the fair, the students worked together to write thank-you letters and provide captions for the photographs that appeared in the school photo album, newsletter, and local newspaper.

An event like this provides an opportunity to invite parents and community members into the school without expecting them to volunteer, purchase items, or donate money.

Celebrating what we know: GOING ON TOUR

With every theme there are always some stories, songs, poems, or activities that the children treasure. "Going on tour" gives them a chance to enjoy their favorites once more and share them with others. Here is an example from one of the author's classes.

1. The teacher and students prepared an information and sign-up sheet, offering to provide entertainment by their class. This was circulated to other classes in the school.

Sign-up sheet and information

2. At the agreed upon times the teacher and the children went to perform at the host classes that signed up. These performances gave the children a wonderful opportunity to polish their skills. As an added bonus, a number of other classes decided to try some of the same activities. One class even decided that it would like to do a similar theme.

Celebrating what we know: PARTY TIME

Sometimes the best way to end a theme is to have a party. One class we know did the following:

1. To end their *Fairy Tale* theme, children made masks and/or simple costumes. The children decided on suitable food and activities for princes, frogs, giants, and wicked stepmothers. (Older children might prefer to use face paints instead of full costumes.)

2. In preparation, the children, with the help of the teacher, made a list of party necessities. Everyone signed up to bring something. With this kind of preplanning there was no waste and no one person had an unreasonable expense. (In schools in which the cost is potentially prohibitive for some families for this type of activity, teachers have managed to find local sponsors.)

3. The school camera was booked for the day of the party to photograph the children wearing the costumes of their favorite characters.

"Tying together" a theme is necessary because it helps us recognize and appreciate the learning that takes place.

How could your children tell, show, or celebrate their learning?

INVITING, INCLUDING, AND INFORMING OTHERS

When we invite, include, and inform others—parents of our students, administrators, and colleagues—we can gain support and enrich our practice.

CONNECTIONS WITH PARENTS: LOOKING AT THE LEARNING

What many parents hear from their children or see them doing at school may seem vastly different from their recollections of the routines and activities they experienced as children. Parents who are included, invited, and informed are more likely to develop an understanding of why you are using themes and to be supportive of what is taking place in the classroom.

The following examples describe three ways of inviting, informing, and including parents.

Parent connections: NEWSLETTERS

Parents appreciate—and sometimes even ask for—newsletters because they help inform them about what their children have done (or will be doing) at school.

Having students help to write the newsletters and prepare material to accompany them make newsletters an even more effective way of communicating.

Some teachers have found it helpful to provide students with frames that become a base for newsletters or supplements to teacher-written newsletters.

Division 12
~ News ~

Our class has developed a real interest in money thanks to Laura's mom designing one of the new Canadian quarters.

After her visit to show the large scale replica of her design the children have been designing their own coins. We have planned two major activities to support their wishes to learn about money.

They are setting up a classroom bank and store and have arranged to visit a local bank (see permission slip attached). If you have any ideas or information or can share we welcome your help.

Thank you,

Colleen and Jennifer

Newsletter from teachers

45

Student-created newsletter

Jessica

Sidney Spit
Wed. June 17th

We leave at

Melissa

8:00 a.m.!

Ashton Please wear
hats

Amy Bring a bag lunch

Lindsey Find out all you can
about cougars.

We will be learning

Heather
more about mammals.

Special thanks to our drivers
Mrs. Dods   Mrs. McFarland
Mrs. Gros   Mrs. Okeefe
Mrs. Leys   Mrs. Payne
We couldn't do it without you!

*Sample frames for child-written
newsletter*

Dear _____ ,

We are doing a theme on _____ .

One activity I enjoyed was _____

_____ .

Two things I've learned are

☆

☆

One thing I still want to find out about is

_____ .

When we started our theme on

_____

I knew _____

_____

_____

Three new things I've learned

☆

☆

☆

But I still wonder about _____

_____

You can help me by _____

_____

_____

You are invited to our

Show What You Know

About _____ Night
(theme)

on _____

from _____ to _____

Come and see how I can

_____

_____

Child's name _____

Reproducible Masters in Appendix A

Parent connections: WORK SAMPLES

If we begin a theme by having children record what they know about a topic, we prepare ourselves for an effective way to share what children have learned. The students first read over their previously prepared list of what they knew before beginning the theme. Then they compile a second list of things they learned about the subject while working on the theme.

Before-and-after journal page

October 5

Sara and José Know that salmon....

are fish
swim in the oshin
come up the river to
spawn
lay eggs
are pink
people eat them
fisherman catsh them.

We could learn more about Salmon...

if I asked my Dad
and by reading books

Signed,
Sara and José

November 10

Now we Know that....
~ not all the eggs srviv
~ baby salmon live under the gravel in the nest.
~ young salmon are called fry
~ they try to make it to the oshin
~ the salmon's nose gets Hooked
~ the mother and father die
~ bears and birds eat the salmon.

The best way for us to learn about salmon was....
~ visiting the river and the nature house and looking at the fish spawn.

Signed,
Sara and José

Parent connections: PICTURES SAY A THOUSAND WORDS

One highly effective way to demonstrate that learning is taking place is to show children in action. During the course of the theme the teacher takes photographs of individual children engaged in various activities. Each child then writes or dictates a caption to accompany the photograph home. These captions open up discussion between the parents and the children as well as provide another connection between parents and the classroom.

In schools in which video cameras are available, teachers can set up the camera for a ten-minute segment that captures students actively involved in learning while working on a theme. The videotape can be signed out overnight or for after-school viewing. This is another way of opening communication between parents and children about the learning that takes place in school.

Photo with student-written caption

Name
philomeNA

Age
6

Date
sept. 23, 1992

I LKe ReCeSS
AND LUNCH AND.
FEE+PlORA+ioN.
AND The TeHes.
AND CA+S

```
┌─────────────────────────────────────────────────────────┐
│                  Parent Response Form                     │
│                                                           │
│  _____ when I watched you on the   │
│        (child's name)                              video  │
│  three things I noticed were...                           │
│                                                           │
│    •                                                      │
│                                                           │
│    •                                                      │
│                                                           │
│    •                                                      │
│                                                           │
│  I also want you to know _____.   │
│                                                           │
│                   Signed _____      │
│                                                           │
└─────────────────────────────────────────────────────────┘
```

Parent response to video

CONNECTIONS WITH ADMINISTRATORS: SUPPORTING THE LEARNING

Like us, our administrators/principals are busy people with specific jobs to accomplish. The best way to help them be supportive of what is happening in our classrooms is to include, invite, and inform them. Some examples of how this can be accomplished are

- ☛ talk to them about what you are doing
- ☛ make sure that they receive a copy of every letter that goes home to parents
- ☛ recognize their expertise, and ask them to act as resource people
- ☛ include them as a possible audience for children's performances and writing

Another effective way to keep administrators informed regarding meeting curriculum goals is to give them an "afterview" at the end of each theme.

The benefits of including, informing, and inviting others easily outweighs the time and energy necessary to extend an invitation or share information. People who feel included can be our best advocates.

What can you do to invite, include, and inform others?

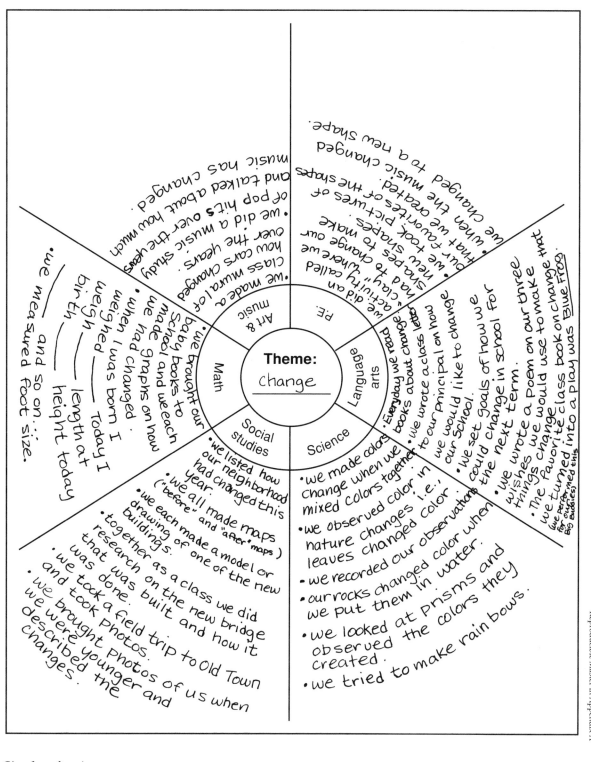

Theme:

Change

Art & music

P.E.

Math

Language arts

Social studies

Science

P.E.
• we took pictures of the shapes that we created.
• we did an activity called "clay," where we had to change our shapes to make new shapes.

Art & music
• we did a music study of pop hits over the years.
• we made a class mural of how cars changed over the years and talked about how much music has changed.

Language arts
• Everyday we read books about change.
• we wrote a class letter to our principal on how we would like to change our school.
• We set goals of how we could change in school for the next term.
• we wrote a poem on our three wishes we would use to make things change.
• The favorite class book on change that we turned into a play was Blue Frog. (We performed this for our Big Buddies.)

Art & music (music changed) / top:
• when I am music changed to a new shape.

Science
• we made color in mixed colors together.
• we observed color in nature changes i.e.; leaves changed color.
• our rocks changed color when we put them in water.
• we looked at prisms and observed the colors they created.
• we tried to make rainbows.

Social studies
• we listed how our neighborhood had changed this year.
• we all made maps ("before" and "after" maps)
• we each made a model or drawing of one of the new buildings.
• together as a class we did research on the new bridge that was built and how it was done.
• we took a field trip to Old Town and took photos.
• we brought photos of us when we were younger and described the changes.

Math
• we measured foot size.
• and so on...
• Today I weigh ___ length at
• When I was born I weighed ___ height today
• birth ___ and ___
• we made graphs on how we had changed.
• we brought our baby books to school and we each weighed ___ height ___

*Circular afterview:
Students had experiences
with numerous activities
connected to **Change** over
the two-week study.*

RESPONDING—QUESTIONS TEACHERS ASK ABOUT WORKING WITH THEMES

Teachers ask many of the same questions about themes. These questions can be grouped around four main headings: time, skills, materials, and choice. As each classroom context is different, we offer suggestions that have worked for us.

How long should a classroom theme last?

A classroom theme may be as short as a couple of days or as long as a month—sometimes even longer. The length of time devoted to a theme is determined by our own interests and beliefs, the learning goals we've established, and the interests of the students.

Remember that even when a theme is officially finished in a classroom, individual children may continue with the theme until their own interest wanes or their questions have been answered.

Sometimes we—the teachers—make the decision to end a theme, while other times we ask for student input. One quick and practical way to assess children's interest is to label two chalkboards, one with "continue" and one with "quit." Children stand in front of the chalkboard that represents their choice. Each tells another child standing in front of the same chalkboard why he or she wants to continue (or conclude) the theme.

An extension to this activity is to have all the children from each section line up facing each other. Each then tells someone from the other side why he or she made that particular choice. Remember, however, that it is the teacher who has the ultimate responsibility for making decisions that affect the learning in the classroom.

How can you find time to use themes in an already over-crowded day?

Themes are not something extra added to an already overcrowded day, but are one way to structure learning experiences. They can actually help make more effective use of class time. However, as themes do require chunks or blocks of time, we've found that it is sometimes necessary to examine our timetable and figure out how we can create large blocks of working time while meeting our curricular responsibilities. Here are three ways that we've adjusted our timetables to incorporate themes.

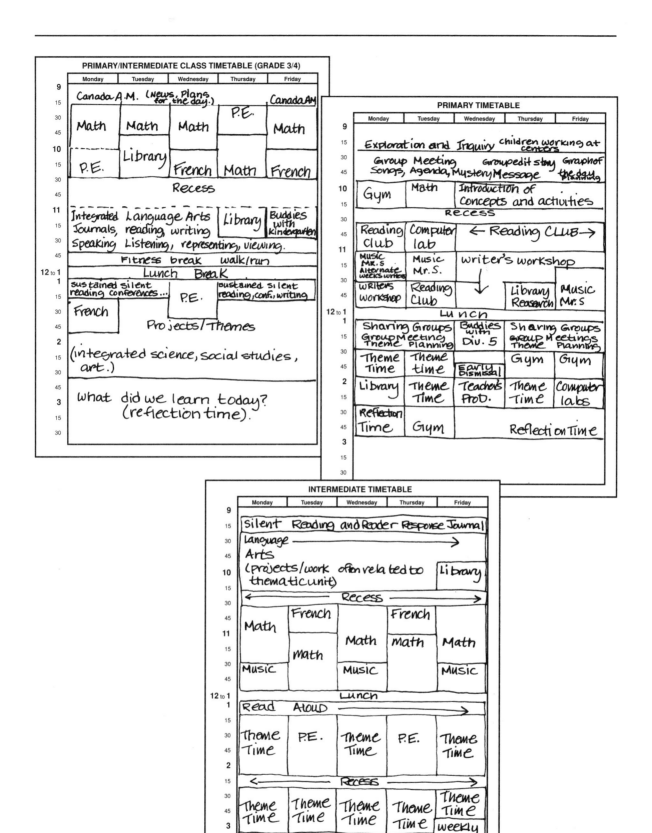

Examples of timetables that incorporate themes

Do themes require more planning time and effort for teachers?

For us this question is connected with examining our role as teachers. When we saw it as our exclusive responsibility to collect all the materials required for a theme, plan all the activities, set up and decorate the classroom, and keep everything organized and attractive, themes took too much time. When we found ourselves working harder than our children, we decided it was time to ask ourselves who was doing the learning. When we realized that much of what we were doing was reducing the number of learning opportunities for our children, we shifted away from the role of teacher as provider.

We found that when we asked our children questions like, "How could we find out about...?" we created a group of co-researchers who could share responsibility for the planning and organization involved with the theme—finding the books, designing the activities, writing letters to invite speakers, collecting supplies, and so on. As well as giving the children a sense of ownership in the learning, we were giving them real reasons to read, write, speak, listen, and the opportunity to practice many more basic skills.

We also had to come to terms with certain issues. For example, bulletin boards created by teams of children may not have matched our expectations, but the learning that took place during their construction was obvious. We realized it wasn't always what we *did* that made the difference, often it was what we *didn't* do.

Are there times when using a theme isn't appropriate?

Yes. Themes are only one way to structure the learning. There are times when we are not involved in a theme because we are planning a new theme, reflecting on what we've learned as a class, or focusing our instructional energies on a specific area such as publishing or mapping skills.

For children who are not used to working with themes, a return to the familiar timetable gives them the opportunity to consolidate their learning. Even in classes where children are accustomed to using themes, a break between themes provides a change of pace, a chance for them to reflect on what they have learned, and an opportunity for them to consider the possibilities for further learning.

The children are certainly having fun, but how do I know that they are really learning?

It is sometimes difficult to see beyond the activities and the fun that the children are having when they are involved in a theme. You may need to uncover what is being learned or practiced to reassure yourself that learning is, indeed, taking place.

If you are looking to see if specific skills are being developed, you could find a curriculum checklist and use a highlighter pen to mark skills that are "uncovered" during the course of the theme.

If you are looking at processes such as writing, reading, or mapping, you could develop your own list of the processes that you want to focus on during the theme-related work, then use this list as you do the curriculum checklist, to determine if your process goals are being met.

It is also important to talk with children about the skills and processes that they are learning and practicing. This helps them know what to tell their parents about their learning. The following example, a web that was sent home in a newsletter to parents, is one way to make the learning involved more obvious for others.

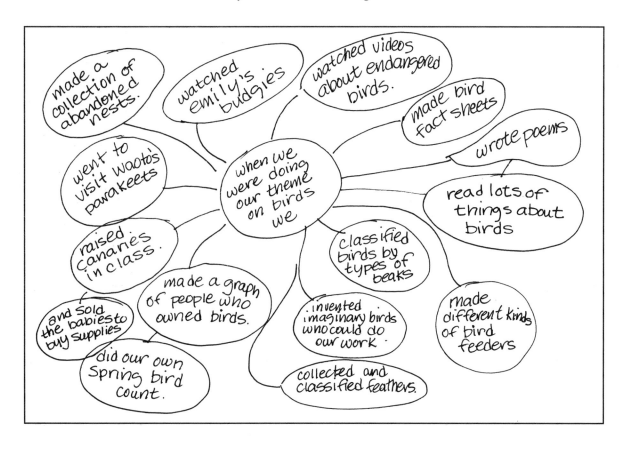

My kids don't all have the same skills, so how can they all work on the same theme?

Themes are an excellent way for children of differing skill levels to learn together. For example, it doesn't matter if children are beginning or advanced readers; each can contribute towards mutual goals.

When we stopped expecting each child to do the same thing at the same time and encouraged children to work on and represent what they had learned in a variety of ways, children of different skill levels were able to work on the same theme. For example, instead of insisting that each child produce a written booklet, we encourage children to represent what they know in a way that works for them. One child may make a model out of plasticine while another will write a journal entry and still another will paint a picture. Teachers can create frameworks to help children record the ways that they can represent their learning. In this way, they are encouraged to expand their repertoires. These frameworks can take the form of a class chart or individual records of the various forms of representation.

What if there are insufficient (or no) materials available for a particular theme?

As long as we subscribe to the notion that all the activities must be planned and all the materials and information must be collected before we can begin a theme, we limit the possibility of capitalizing on the students' interests. For example, the lack of library books available on oil spills should not stop a theme about oil spills from getting started.

One way to include children in sharing the responsibility for collecting and gathering resource materials is to create a list at the

---

Sombrio
Name

My way of representing/showing what I know

Date	Event
Oct. 17	I made a poster showing the orbits of the planets around the sun.
Nov. 4	I wrote a story for my little buddy.
Dec. 15	I acted in our 'readers theater'
Jan. 9.	I made a tape of my research report on space to put in the Library
Jan. 21	I wrote a letter to the newspaper about people in cars speeding by our school.
Jan. 30.	I wrote a letter to my pen pal and drew a picture of our school!
Feb. 2	I made a diorama of the race in the book Stone Fox.
Feb. 16	Elijah, Leon, and I made a play about meeting Captain Cook.
Mar. 3	I talked about my thinking as I did a math problem on the board.

Informal record of learning

Reproducible Master in Appendix A

beginning of any theme noting all the resources that would support that theme. For example, as teachers we may ask, "How could we find out about whales?" Children could then suggest all the different ways they could think of to find out about whales. Teachers may choose to keep the list posted in the class and have children sign their names whenever they contribute.

Having limited resources may appear to be a roadblock to working with children on a theme, but in the long run it may prove to be a benefit. A lack of materials forces us to ask our students, their parents, our colleagues, and administrators for help. Request letters may be sent home to parents outlining lists of things that would be useful. One staff posts blank chart paper in the staff room each month. Teachers record on it the themes that their classes are involved in, and make requests for contributions. (See facing page.)

We're trying to find out information about _____.
(theme)

Who can bring…?

records/tapes	visitors	home videos
_____	_____	_____
_____	_____	_____
_____	_____	_____
_____	_____	_____
books	**ideas**	**collections**
_____	_____	_____
_____	_____	_____
_____	_____	_____
_____	_____	_____
pictures	**magazines**	**ingredients for—**
_____	_____	_____
_____	_____	_____
_____	_____	_____
_____	_____	_____
arts and crafts	**supplies**	**treasures**
_____	_____	_____
_____	_____	_____
_____	_____	_____
_____	_____	_____

Sign-up chart

Reproducible Master in Appendix A

Thanks for all
the materials gang!
we're ready now.
     John

Our kids have
gone crazy about
money — does
anybody have
any coin
stamps?
or ?.?
Jen +
Colleen

Help! I need
information and
books and ???
about Spiders!
Sue

We're off and running
with a Chris Van Allsburg
'unit.' Can we borrow
your books? Do you have
any other materials
that might help us out?
Jan

DOES ANYONE HAVE
ANY BOOKS ON LOGGING?
André

With the explosion of knowledge in our rapidly changing world, no one teacher can collect or know all there is to know about a subject. Failing to collect all the materials in advance of a theme can provide an ideal opportunity for students to become actively engaged in seeking information for real purposes.

How much choice do students have in selecting and planning themes?

When we, as teachers, offer choices, we make sure that they are educationally sound and are appropriate within our classroom context. For example, we would not ask a three-year-old to tell us what he wanted for breakfast. Instead we ask whether he wants porridge, cold cereal, or scrambled eggs. If the choice for the class has to do with ways in which students could represent what they learned about insects, for example, teachers may ask, "How would you like to represent this—a poster, a labeled model, or a picture collage?"

The most important point is that children have some opportunity for input into the theme. The degree will vary depending on the children, your own comfort level, and the goals you've set.

Student input may take place at the beginning of the theme when you are deciding what the theme will be, it may be when students help select books that they want to read on the topic, or it may come when students have some choice as to how they represent what they have learned. It may be in *all* those aspects as long as the choices we offer are educationally sound and are appropriate within our classroom context.

Do you have any suggestions for theme topics?

As we have indicated in chapter 2—and throughout this book—possibilities for theme topics are almost unlimited. Topics can be predetermined or can develop quite spontaneously. This may be as a result of such things as a book that students have read or something that happens at school—perhaps by something a child has brought into class, something that happens at an activity center, or something triggered by a classroom quest.

It has been our experience that when we organize themes around broad ideas rather than specific topics, there is a greater scope for all individuals to pursue areas that are of interest and relevance to them. However, we also know that a theme on a subject as far-reaching as the environment can be treated superficially, while children can turn a theme on pets into an in-depth investigation. Therefore, we believe that there are no "good" or "bad" themes.

The only way to judge the suitability of any given theme idea is by determining whether or not a particular theme has potential for helping your students to learn!

Here is a potpourri of theme ideas that we have found particularly successful:

- Changes
- Questions
- Water
- Color
- Patterns
- Connections
- Relationships
- Living things
- Collections
- Sports
- Treasures
- Nature secrets
- Communities
- Travels
- Books
- Characters
- Writing
- Thinking

- Showing what we know
- Environment
- Homes
- Growing
- Families
- Friendships
- Learning
- Wellness

As we work with children and themes we continue to ask ourselves what's working? What's not? What's next?

Asking questions is how we learn and grow. As you reflect on your experiences using themes, you will create new questions, and as you work together with your children, parents, and colleagues you will compose your own answers.

What questions do you have now?

Who could you connect with to discover the answers you need?

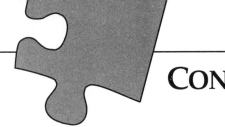

CONCLUSION

We include *Building Connections* in our title because we recognize how important making connections is to everyone's learning. Just as there are ways to encourage children to make connections, we invite you to make your own connections between your past experiences and your present practices, between what you are doing now and what you want to do—between and among you and your children, colleagues, and administrators, and with the parents of your students and your community. As you read this book, each of you has made different connections. There is no right or wrong connection; there is no "state of higher connectedness." What is important is that you have built connections that make sense for you.

We want you to recognize the expert that *you* have within yourself and recognize that *you* are able to construct the knowledge you need around the issue of themes. Use the ideas that work for you. Adapt them, change them—make them your own. In this way you can make themes work for you and your children within the context of your school community.

We enjoy conducting workshops and institutes. If you would like further information we invite you to write us:

> c/o Peguis Publishers
> 520 Hargrave Street
> Winnipeg, Manitoba
> Canada R3A 0X8

APPENDIX—
REPRODUCIBLE MASTERS

A

What do you already know about _____ ?	What do you wonder about _____ ?	How can we find out answers to some of our questions?

Page 9: "Getting Started"
chart

Page 14: Cross-examination form

Language Arts—Reading, Writing, Listening, Speaking, Viewing

Social Studies
Physical Education
Art
Music

ACADEMIC SUBJECTS →

GOALS →

Mathematics
Science
Library
Computers
Family Life

Intellectual, Physical, Social, Emotional, and Artistic Development

TEACHER REFLECTIONS

This theme has possibilities because…

GUIDE QUESTIONS

- Is this theme relevant to children?

- Are there opportunities for connections?

- Will it generate enthusiasm/enjoyment?

- Does it allow for student choice and a range of interests, abilities, and strengths?

- Is it a good use of our time?

- Are there real questions to be answered and a real audience for the answers?

- Does it give children the opportunity to use a variety of learning processes?

- What curriculum content and processes does this theme address?

Page 21: Teacher's preliminary web

_____ Month _____

Skills and Processes	Week of	Week of	Week of	Week of

Skills taught in the context of student work

I means you work with an individual or individuals/
    maybe in a conference as you talk with them about their writing

W is a whole class activity

G is for a group of children that you
    brought together for the same skill

*Page 27: "Curriculum
Connections" form*

Theme				
Focus				
Date				

Page 28: Observing and recording children's learning

To show what I know about _____
(theme)

I _____
(made a model, wrote a poem, drew a picture...)

Three things I want you to notice are

•

•

•

One thing I learned today

about _____
(theme)

that I could teach someone

at home is _____

_____

_____

_____

Date _____ Theme _____

Here is a photo of me working

with _____

```
(place photo here)
```

When we work together we can _____

_____

Two things that _____
(theme)

make me think about are

•

•

Name _____

Theme _____

Three things that I learned from my friends when we studied

_____
(theme)

are...

•

•

•

Pages 31, 32: Frames for children's self-evaluation

Dear _____ ,
(teacher)

If you do this theme on _____
with another class I would suggest that you could
make it better by

  1.

  2.

  3.

The other thing I'd like to tell you is _____

_____

              signed _____

Name _____

Theme _____

Three things my friends would
say that they learned from me
when we studied

_____
                    (theme)

are…

•

•

•

Name _____

Date _____

Before we started to learn

about _____

I used to think _____

_____

_____

Now I think _____

_____

_____

When we studied _____

my favorite _____
                  (visitor, book, video, film)

was _____.

This is a picture of what I liked.

              by _____

From: Building Connections: *Making Themes Work* by Davies/Politano/Cameron © 1993. May be reproduced for classroom use.

Pages 31, 32: Frames for
children's self-evaluation

Theme _____ Name _____

I wonder about the answers to these three questions

•

•

•

I could try to find out the answers by

•

•

The one thing I will remember

about _____
        (theme)

long after our study is over is

_____

_____

_____

Theme _____

Things I learned from...

Books

People

Other

by _____

Books on our theme

_____

I heard   I looked at   I read

My all-time favorite is

_____

Pages 31, 32: Frames for children's self-evaluation

THEME PORTFOLIO INDEX

_____

_____

_____

_____

_____

_____

_____

_____

_____

_____

_____

_____

_____

_____

_____

_____

_____

_____

_____

Page 33: Theme
portfolio index

The summary spiral, reading from the center outward:

When we first started this theme I thought

(theme)

I wondered

I found out that

Something else that I can share with others is

I still wonder about

One more thing I want you to know is

Page 39: Summary spiral

COMPLIMENT CARD FOR _____

☆

☆

COMPLIMENT CARD FOR _____

☆

☆

COMPLIMENT CARD FOR _____

☆

☆

Page 40: Compliment card

When we started our theme on

_____

I knew _____

_____

_____

Three new things I've learned

☆

☆

☆

But I still wonder about _____

_____

You can help me by _____

_____

_____

Dear _____ ,

We are doing a theme on _____ .

One activity I enjoyed was _____

_____ .

Two things I've learned are

☆

☆

One thing I still want to find out about is

_____ .

You are invited to our

Show What You Know

About _____ Night
(theme)

on _____

from _____ to _____

Come and see how I can

_____

_____

Child's name _____

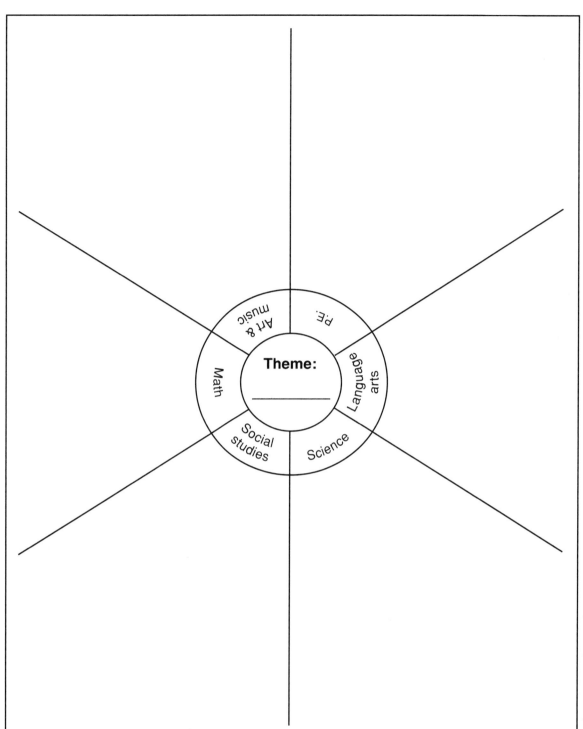

Theme:
_____

Art & music

P.E.

Language arts

Science

Social studies

Math

Page 50: Circular afterview

_____
Name

My way of representing/showing
what I know

Date	Event

We're trying to find out information about_____.

(theme)

Who can bring...?

records/tapes

_____
_____
_____
_____
_____

visitors

_____
_____
_____
_____
_____

home videos

_____
_____
_____
_____
_____

books

_____
_____
_____
_____

ideas

_____
_____
_____
_____

collections

_____
_____
_____
_____

pictures

_____
_____
_____
_____

magazines

_____
_____
_____
_____

ingredients for—

_____
_____
_____
_____

arts and crafts

_____
_____
_____
_____

supplies

_____
_____
_____
_____

treasures

_____
_____
_____
_____

Page 56: Sign-up chart

APPENDIX — SUGGESTED READING

Bosak, Susan, and A. Gower. *Science Is.* Richmond Hill, ON: Scholastic, 1986.

Brownlie, Faye, Susan Close, and Linda Wingren. *Reaching for Higher Thought.* Edmonton, AB: Arnold Publishing, 1988.

Caine, Renate Nummela, and Geoffrey Caine. *Making Connections: Teaching and the Human Brain.* Alexandria, VA: Association for Supervision and Curriculum Development, 1991.

Davies, Anne, Caren Cameron, Colleen Politano, and Kathleen Gregory. *Together Is Better: Collaborative Assessment, Evaluation and Reporting.* Winnipeg, MB: Peguis Publishers, 1992.

Harste, Jerome, and Kathy Short. *Creating Classrooms for Authors.* Portsmouth, NH: Heinemann, 1988.

Johnson, Terry, and Daphne Louis. *Bringing It All Together.* Richmond Hill, ON: Scholastic, 1990.

———. *Literacy Through Literature.* Richmond Hill, ON: Scholastic, 1987.

Barrell, John. *Teaching for Thoughtfulness: Classroom Strategies to Enhance Intellectual Development.* New York: Longman, 1991.

Pigdon, Keith, and Marilyn Woolley, eds. *The Big Picture: Integrating Children's Learning.* Armadale, Australia: Eleanor Curtain Publishing, 1992.

Short, Kathy, and Carolyn Burke. *Creating Curriculum: Teachers and Students as a Community of Learners.* Portsmouth, NH: Heinemann, 1991.

Smith, Frank. *To Think.* New York: Teachers College Press, Columbia University, 1990.

Tchudi, Stephen. *Travels Across the Curriculum: Models for Interdisciplinary Learning.* Bright Ideas Series. Richmond Hill, ON: Scholastic, 1991.